more than here

J V Birch

# more than here

## Acknowledgements

'Auntie Australia' in *The Emma Press Anthology of Aunts* (UK), 2017
'Blackberrying' in *Foxglove Journal* (UK), 2017
'Ladybirds' in *Transnational Literature*, Flinders University (Australia), 2018
'Catch up' in *Transnational Literature*, Flinders University (Australia), 2016
'Coffin Bay' in *Plumwood Mountain* (Australia), 2017
'Bird watching' in *Foxglove Journal* (UK), 2017
'Silver brumby' in *Wild*, Ginninderra Press (Australia), 2017
'Because' in *Grieve* Volume 5 from Hunter Writers Centre (Australia), 2018
'Endoscopy Unit' in *Ponder Review* (US), 2017
'Masks' in *The Poetry Shed* (UK), 2018
'Pay back' in *First Refuge: Poems on Social Justice*, Ginninderra Press (Australia), 2016
'Balinese pool' in *Foxglove Journal* (UK), 2017
'Bordertown' in *Tincture Journal* (Australia), 2016
'Flight attendant' in *Tamba* (Australia), 2018

## Thanks

I would like to thank my poetry groups – Poetica, East Avenue Books, Jan Owen and fellow members – and the Poetry School – tutors Clare Shaw, David Tait and Claire Trévien, and fellow students – for their invaluable feedback on several of the poems in this collection.

And thank you to my husband Andreas for giving me the time and space to do what I love – you take me to places.

*more than here*
ISBN 978 1 76041 693 5
Copyright © text J V Birch 2019
Cover photograph: J V Birch

First published 2019 by
**Ginninderra Press**
PO Box 3461 Port Adelaide 5015 Australia
www.ginninderrapress.com.au

# Contents

| | |
|---|---|
| Recall the tenderness of us | 9 |
|   Flame | 11 |
|   Auntie Australia | 12 |
|   Blackberrying | 13 |
|   Leap | 14 |
|   Waiting for the steam train to Bridgenorth | 15 |
|   Monster leaves | 16 |
|   Going back to Greensleeves | 17 |
|   Ladybirds | 18 |
|   Of the men in my life | 19 |
|   Catch up | 20 |
|   Huntress | 21 |
|   Click, slide, click | 22 |
|   Rivers | 23 |
|   Boomerang | 24 |
| Feel the sting of a long-ago star | 25 |
|   Bayside | 27 |
|   Elephant | 28 |
|   Fox | 29 |
|   Moon jellyfish | 30 |
|   Coffin Bay | 31 |
|   Birdwatching | 32 |
|   Ibises | 33 |
|   Golden orb | 34 |
|   High Street, Bromsgrove | 35 |
|   Maritime bear | 36 |
|   Weddell seal | 37 |
|   Duck à la Noosa | 38 |
|   Blackbird | 39 |

|  |  |
|---|---|
| Southern right whales | 40 |
| Lamniform lullaby | 41 |
| Silver brumby | 42 |

## Take over your life and be — 43

|  |  |
|---|---|
| Because | 45 |
| What stays with you | 46 |
| primordial | 47 |
| Kissing Japan | 48 |
| Land of Ice | 49 |
| Endoscopy Unit | 50 |
| Masks | 51 |
| Hands | 52 |
| 7 July 2005 & after | 53 |
| The Terracotta Army | 54 |
| The Suicide Net | 55 |
| Shop no. 4 | 56 |
| City to Seaford | 57 |
| Pay back | 58 |
| Reef fishing | 59 |
| Balinese pool | 60 |

## Run with the colours of home — 61

|  |  |
|---|---|
| Interislander | 63 |
| City of cones | 64 |
| Bordertown | 65 |
| Jaipur | 66 |
| Fox Glacier | 67 |
| Adelaide vs Brisbane | 68 |
| Jantar Mantar | 70 |
| Snowdonia | 71 |
| Bondi to Bronte | 72 |
| The Oodnadatta Track | 73 |

| | |
|---|---:|
| The Taj | 75 |
| Henley Beach | 76 |
| Flight attendant | 77 |
| Sólfar, Reykjavik | 78 |
| Mahjong | 79 |
| Darwinian | 80 |

I work very hard and I play very hard. I'm grateful for life. And I live it. I believe life loves the liver of it. I live it.

Maya Angelou

# Recall the tenderness of us

# Flame

Curved glass is split into panels
each holds a pair of hearts
one big
one small
dappled red and beating
against a backdrop of midnight.

I think of your arms around me
how when the world's winds flux
in the wild dark falling
you quiet our corner
as we watch the tealight flicker
pool itself.

# Auntie Australia

It's Sunday night, Skype time
and I feel the smile as my brother appears,
his son perched on his lap.

*This is daddy's sister, your auntie in Australia.*
And that's how it started – 'Auntie Australia' –
my nephew clapping and grinning.

I notice his lashes have grown,
his eyes are bluer, he's got a new tooth.
I attempt a screenshot – like netting a butterfly

as he plays with the keys,
sees himself in the corner of the screen,
beams and waves, looks back up at his dad.

We swap news of our fingertip family.
And after goodbyes, as their image disappears,
Charlie's grin is suspended, bridging

the distance, last to leave like the Wonderland cat's.

# Blackberrying

We walk along the river in Arrowtown
from full sun to hollow shade to welcome shadow.

Trees hum with a green to remember
as the shallow water trips and twists over rock bed.

We find the fat little jewels of blackberries
race back to our childhoods as we share each bounty
kiss clean one another's purple-stained fingers
recall the tenderness of us.

# Leap

You planned our trip
while I tried to grow up faster,
the furthest I'd ever been was Spain with family.

I swapped suitcase for rucksack
& practised packing
to be the self-composed girl you fell for.

Departure day arrived.
I rose early, lacking sleep,
sick with nerves three cups of tea couldn't calm.

The long tube ride seemed short,
Heathrow a haze, but
I remember hot chips & you saying you loved me.

My flight was a thin stretch of panicked naps,
yours full of film, food, fitful rest.
When the screen showed us over Delhi

I felt hysteria rising,
told myself to breathe,
that I was with you & would return a woman.

# Waiting for the steam train to Bridgenorth

I'm so cold I can feel my bones.

We're the only ones at the station
this early on a Sunday.
It's still dark, but the sun's yawning.

I pretend I'm a mini steam engine
and puff out my breath –
baby clouds gone in a blink.

I look at my new family.

My dad, brother and stepbrother
don't seem to mind the cold,
boys wrapped up in dreams of machines
swapping figures and facts to pass time.
Nan is sat silent and folded in furs,
my stepmum's the same, but has bite.

Then it suddenly gets warmer
as Gramps steps behind me
and draws me into his coat.

Now I don't mind the wait.

# Monster leaves

I remember the first time I saw one.
Walking from the tube down Bermondsey Street
it was crouched on the pavement
a maple leaf
as big as my hand
with sharp-toothed edges.
I swear I heard it roar.

The home projects we had as children
(once the new wife had moved in)
you chose birds
our stepbrother insects
and I had trees.
If I'd found this back then
I'd have been favourite for a while.

# Going back to Greensleeves

I'm in my Nan's garden
a sprawling country of colour
split into states
lawn, vegetable, orchard.
Sheep bleat in the field next door
like memories on legs.
I remember being happy here
barefoot among daisies
twirling in one of my Nan's old dresses
she'd downsized for me.
She helped my imagination leave its room
and soar into the blue.
I have my Nan's eyes.
Will she know me when it's my time?
A butterfly settles on the rockery
seesaws its wings as if trying to balance.
I'll see her again, I can pin her curls.
I head towards the trees –
the apples need picking.

# Ladybirds

I try to call you every three weeks to conjure you again.
Today's a good day, with your morning and my evening,

we span the in-between. You ask about me –
how I've been, my husband, my work – and I share,

like this is routine. I reciprocate, mention your heatwave
blazing across our wintered news. You say it's been hot,

but not a patch on the summer after I was born,
the hottest on record and when the ladybirds came.

You tell me again how you didn't know what to do
with me, tried to keep me cool by putting my pram

in the shade veiled in white cotton. I try to picture you
cooing and fanning to keep me appeased, and can't.

Instead, I see a rippling swathe of ladybirds, a delicate
sea of red, lifting their skirts for any promise of breeze.

# Of the men in my life

When my now husband told me he was
falling in love with me, I was turning fish fingers,
juggling the phone and tongs as he relayed

an event from his day, dropping it in as a fact.
He doesn't tell me he loves me often,
but when he does, it has a certain weight,

not the slip of a thing from those before him
who felt the need to say it whenever we spoke.
I think back to my dad who preferred to give

praise than affection, until he met a woman
who made it bloom, as though it'd been waiting
for good weather. I remember his last shave,

how my brother helped, gentle with the razor
as if it was blade not electric, and my dad
stretching down his top lip so my brother

could reach under his nose. My nephew said
*I miss you* last Sunday in one of our regular
Skype sessions, my brother alongside him,

my husband beside me. It was Father's Day.

# Catch up

I remember walking through London with you.
We'd shared a bottle of wine at the Euston Flyer
though the naff kind
(since moving down under
I'd become a connoisseur).
We were raw
visceral
stripped back to our bones.
And we talked about Dad
about your breaking and my falling
about the space of him in our lives.
We bled a little
peeling back years
prodding old wounds
in real time.

## Huntress

Returning from the bathroom, I settle next to him
who's not snoring for a change so I'm liking
him near me. The room seems full of slumber.

Then I hear it, the high-pitched whine by my ear.
I wave it away with ridiculous hate. It comes back
again & again, a dive-bomber on a mission.

When it tip-touches my cheek, I know it has to go.
*Dammit* I mutter & snap on the light, find it surprisingly
quickly, clinging to the lampshade on his side.

I advance with a tissue, my final move swift
causing a tiny explosion of red. Barely lifting from

sleep, he calls me his little huntress & I smile,
spoon against the length of his back, feed off his

heat, dream I'm a panther, stalking, fearless.

# Click, slide, click

I see it & hear *click, slide, click*. He stands
with a briefcase between his feet – shined

shoes, tucked shirt, hair trimmed close,
swaying in rhythm with the train, intent

on a book about fighter jets – oblivious
to the memory that's pin-tailed me back.

To you, striding important in suits, with perfect
knot ties under your aftershave swathe, neat

when you leave & loose on return, brisk but
warm in your goodbyes & hellos, before heading

for the custard cream biscuits. You, always
in hand with your black leather case & its

sun-stunned locks, into which, if I'm lucky
to be close when you *click, slide, click*, I steal

a look at what you carry so well – pens, papers,
notebooks, folders – all in place like I used to be.

# Rivers

There's a river
   in me & a
      river in you
         & mostly
           they flow
              in different
                 directions
                    cos that's
                       how it is
                          with you
                       & me but
                    there's a
                  place that
                shores them
              both where
           you centre
         me & I flow
      into your
     flowing
    returning
  us to the
beginning
 when I
  reached
     out & you
       reached
         back &
            we swam
               in the deep
                   & the shallows

# Boomerang

You see Tuesday's
sun after me

I gift it
with your name

When I breakfast
on Friday

you snore soft
in pyjamas

twitch in your step
over midnight

With Sunday coffee
& a photo of me

you kiss my smile
good morning

as I taste stars
leaping miles to you

**Feel the sting of a long-ago star**

## Bayside

And then a bat

        swoops from a tree

                its wingspan sharp

                & the length of you

        bears down for a beat

broad & brooding

        like something not said

                before losing its impact

                pinwheeling away

        to punctuate the sky

with its dark

# Elephant

The heat was exhausting and we'd seen nothing for days.
None of the daily leopard, rhino or lion sightings
mocking us on the map in reception.

Some hippos from a distance
freezing our asses on a twilight tour to spot 'the big three',
but otherwise, in Kruger, nothing.

Driving back to our lodge into the sun on its knees
we start to snipe, exchanging hot words,
both of us testy and tired.

And then, without warning, a heavy-footed eclipse
inches away, the hulk of it moving with purpose and thought,
ears flapping, trunk waving – *I'm here, see me, see me!*

# Fox

Walking home late one evening
streets deep in nocturnal hum
I turn a corner and see it
picking through split rubbish bags.
Drawn and thin
its fur is dark
so far from the blaze
of its full-bodied hunted other.
It looks up
spots me watching
its *tapetum lucidum* brilliant
as a bus rumbles by.

## Moon jellyfish

A rippling sheet of blue beckons
with a rhythm divided.

Slim fish dart swift hellos
over shells both hollow and whole

the ridged bed a haven for hard heels.
Circles of shadow stipple the surface.

I peer closer. A smattering of jellyfish
pulsate like shallow water galaxies

some the size of a fingernail
others could cover a palm

and I dare myself to cup one
feel the sting of a long-ago star.

# Coffin Bay

Crayfish, pilchards,
ocean jackets and sharks

Octopus, sea urchins,
sea snails and scallops

Sand crabs, abalone,
garfish and whiting

Shush
the oysters are sleeping.

# Birdwatching

I watch a pair of lorikeets gorge on overripe peaches. They hook the ample flesh with their beaks chattering between mouthfuls, their green the green of the leaves so only the vivid blue of their heads is visible, with an occasional blaze of breast. I think of the women at the café in Brighton. Every Sunday they sit at a table by the window with their tea and cream cakes, heads bent in gossip, oblivious to their surrounds and smeared lips. At that time, in their world, it's just them. I note the quiet, feel watched, look up to find the parrots staring at me, a couple of plump sunsets untouched at their feet.

# Ibises

Slurping our ice creams in the shade –
yours rum and raisin, mine forever

chocolate – we watch the ibises
stepping with care between picnickers.

They're quirky birds, reminiscent of taps,
drink from the remnants of one,

angling their heads so their beaks
are upside down, the only way they can

get close enough to pincer the pool.
A young boy rushes them – they scatter

like some poor man's flamenco.
One shoots him a backward glance,

as if sizing him up.

# Golden orb

The ride is downhill on near-death bikes.
We can choose the gentle route
or a challenging off-road one.
I opt for ease, tail Putu, my young guide,
with a girl from Hong Kong,
while the rest bounce & bruise elsewhere.

Ten minutes in Putu brings us to a stop,
strides up to a tree to grab something,
returns with a fist full of nightmare.
Akiko screams, I swear, at the monstrous thing,
all legs & no sense.
Putu dangles it like a yo-yo as it tries to thread its escape,
its body as big as my thumb.
*What you making fuss for?*
*You not want to hold, no?*

The others skid up with shrieks & gasps,
snap photos from a distance with zoom.
A Polish girl endures its tiptoe on her arm,
quite likes it, declares love, attempts a mock kiss,
until it scales her head to tread yellow tresses,
spinning as if it's come home.

# High Street, Bromsgrove

I remember my surprise
seeing it skitter across the bitumen.

It was a November afternoon
cold enough for hats and gloves.

I was leaving my favourite shop
the sort you can lose yourself in

spend yourself silly
its bell above the door sounding my exit.

Stepping down to the pavement
a thin movement caught my eye –

a house spider dashing across the road
as if it had somewhere to be.

# Maritime bear

With midnight skin hidden under thick
dense fur, he glows brightest in the Arctic
ring of life as he ambles along polynyas.

He is *ice bear uncle* to circumpolar
people, a spiritual and cultural being
of lumbering gait, fat legs and small ears.
And yet he's a fantastical beauty,
with wide feet and scooped claws
perfect for snow, propulsive in paddle,
paw pads bumped with soft black papillae.

Revered, solitary, cautious and fatal,
he's a keystone species serving Arctic
foxes his leftovers. And in love with seals,
who torture him with their annual absence,
their number balancing his in an
evolutionary dance of claw and blubber,
blubber and claw, until climate change cuts in.

He stops abruptly in all his majestic maleness,
his senses brilliant, caught on a whiff of seal
– ringed or bearded – its scent bursting colour
behind his eyes. He hasn't eaten for days,
his hunger an eight-foot growl loathe to risk
another vertical drop in howling weather
for the odd egg, blind chick, if lucky, both.

So the still-hunt begins as the light fades.
He crouches beside the breathing hole,
becomes the silence, the snow, the ice

polynya – a stretch of open water surrounded by ice.
papillae – small dermal bumps.

# Weddell seal

*It lives on ice shelves around Antarctica*
we're told
*further south on the planet than any other mammal.*
*The known record for holding its breath is ninety-six minutes.*

The video's on a loop
opens with an empty breathing hole.
Impossibly blue water rocks before up it pops
in a cold gasp
drawing lungfuls of breath for all its worth.
It has an old baby face
with liquid black eyes and a Mona Lisa smile
like it knows what we don't.

*Looks like a fat puddin' ready for bakin'*
a tourist sniggers to another.
*Glasshouses* I think
and step towards this circle of life.

# Duck à la Noosa

We have the pool to ourselves,
with the exception of the duck
on the island under the banana tree.

You attempt to engage with a series
of quacks. It ruffles its feathers,
shakes its head – I swear it rolls its eyes.

We circle the island slowly as it circles
the other way, a synchronised dance
of pale toes and webbed feet.

And then, with a splash, its off,
a neat brown bundle bobbing
on blistering blue, paddling hard.

It reaches an edge as we tread water,
watching, and with a wing-lifted hop
it's up and out, flapping to a roof,

flinging off chlorine.

# Blackbird

There's a cascading chorus
from the old oak tree
where you find a feathered
shadow shuffling inside.

With yellow-ringed eyes
it blinks and peers back
like a second morning
as you sip your sugared tea.

It's a complicated tumble
of warbles, twitters and chirps,
mostly repeated precisely,
rarely with a detectable change.

And you feel that sweet pull
at the back of your throat
as if you want to join in,
sing your heart out across the sky.

# Southern right whales

We drive to Basham Beach where they've been sighted
the most and from the viewing platform,

catch the weight of their shadow anchored in breakers
some hundred metres off shore.

*A mother and her calf* an enthusiast grins, and I narrow
my eyes, zoom my camera to max,

trying to catch the hulk of them, find only the promise
of something. Disappointed, we head

to Victor Harbor for ice cream, walk to Granite Island,
the crossing littered with tourists

and the old horse-drawn tram. Heading home, and because
it's en route, I suggest we stop by

the beach again. Plunging to the shoreline, I fall back to child
hollering *there they are, there they are!*

within swimming distance and blowing hello, breaching the blue
like islands come home.

# Lamniform lullaby

I am nowhere you want to be
and the greatest around
with the exception of only one other.

I will live the length of your life
can shake yours from you
and make you everywhere at once.

My teeth will serrate your sleep
my stare will split your mind
just my being will quicken your blood.

I will swoop on your heartbeat
drag it down to the rest
hunt hard and fast like a silver blade.

I am the coast of your island
in the depth you will know
I can give you the dark and forever.

# Silver brumby

Hunted for the moon in his coat
he looks downriver
from tumbled rocks

like some sure-footed god

Wild and gleaming
he listens to what the wind
tells him

reads the snowgrass and skies
makes a deal
with the coming storm

that he will lead its lightning
when they track closer
make them believe

they chase nothing but a ghost

**Take over your life and be**

# Because

you've gone Dad, I'm arranging a new one,
mending myself to you piece by fabricated piece.

I begin with your feet, position your once white
trainers so you're surveying the back garden,

what to trim and weed. Next, the grass-stained,
paint-splattered jeans you wore at weekends

to do odd jobs around the house, which always
took you longer than planned. To finish, a red

sweater that hints of you, even now. All you
need is a little life. Closing the wardrobe,

I swear I see your foot twitch, picture you smiling
at me like the last time I saw you, which I knew

would be the last. I tie your laces, just in case.

# What stays with you

I grew up on a crescent
in a house with matching front door and garage
and a carport pole I peeled black paint from.
There was a barometer in the hallway
which could never fathom our weather
and each room was colour-schemed with nothing out of place
except maybe us children.
Afternoon tea was always at four
in cups on saucers angled with spoons
and our eyes on the biscuits, waiting.

Now I'm on the other side of the world
in a home set back from a tree-lined street.
A potted palm thrives whatever the weather
waves me inside where there's sunlit space
and although clean and tidy, it breathes.
My favourite time of day is still late afternoon
but on the sofa outside with a glass of wine and my thoughts
where between bursts of lorikeets
there are pockets of sea scent
and a sky of immeasurable blue.

# **primordial**

it's out there beyond our vision
tracks us by the width of day
a measure of moon
the space in between
notes how we work our land our stock our time
slick in our sweat & grease & snot

                                it puts the cold in our hearts
                                    & the rocks in our blood
                            makes each thud an unwanted thing
                              it compels us to undo our doing
              leave our fear in our boots for the dogs to mind
                        it waits as we turn wild with waiting

then when night is punctured with eyes
& we've plundered ourselves
it calls to the dark in us
where shadows have breath & bone
& with one swift move
brings the absence of everything

# **Kissing Japan**

Shaking            to break me      apart
       you shove
               then slip hard
beneath my weight

Your silence      means danger
       a moment of still
                  like a caring horror
before you whip back the cover
             to surprised tender depths

Nowhere to go     I wait
       for you to rise
                 and humble us all

And as you claim my chest
              my neck
                  my face
       I steal a kiss
from your jellyfished lips

# Land of Ice

## Then

Cold buried into bone, shattered marrow and snowflaked
the skin, caused extremities to lose all sense
of themselves. Dark was a promised thing that fell
wildly, indifferent to time. The winds hungered, returned
everything home. Death became too close in the walls,
made breath bleed, undo itself.

## Now

Ahead lies the Blue Lagoon to still shivered bones. Crossing
its shore, our goose-bumped bodies tip-touch
snow & ice. Plumes of steam soften the glittering granite
as mountains watch, silent. When the pool's edge is lipped,
we slip off our shelter, step into the milky blue, blissfully
unaware of what lies below.

# Endoscopy Unit

Pyjamaed in greens
I quickly learn what to do.

How to thread steady when taking a biopsy
not change expression when bad news is found
sterilise equipment for the next insertion
calm the patient who didn't sleep last night
clean up the one who had breakfast that morning
search for polyps in waste before lunch.

But a DNR is tricky.
I remember my first to be also my last.

The death mid-scope
the final time call
prepping the body for the family farewell.

This they can't teach.

# Masks

I never had the chance to give you the masks
we bought you from The Gambia. Leaving gifts

to last minute, we wearied a market with the midday
sun, intent on finding you something among

the rainbow of dresses, the hand-painted bowls,
the ivory nobody wants anymore. And then

I saw them – heavy lidded, full lips, slender
noses, one male, the other less so – exquisitely

carved in dark wood. I knew you'd like them,
would examine them slowly, even feel the African

heat in your palm. We came back on a Thursday
and I called you the next day to tell you about our trip.

I asked how you were. You said you hadn't been feeling
yourself, that it was probably nothing. On Sunday you rang

from a hospital, in with suspected gall stones, a bladder
that may have to come out. And then it all happened quickly.

Tests revealed shadows – the secondary found first,
the primary after – a diagnosis was given but no time.

You died. In seven days. At home. In your sleep.
I never had the chance to give you the masks

we bought you from The Gambia. Think this when I see
them on the wall in our study. A world away, like you.

# Hands

I was queuing at college when it happened,
examining my hands, thinking how pale they were, with
some nails missing their moons.

A rising murmur became a torrent of words became
a wave of shock, free-flowing anguish for those known
and for those not.

In my session after, the tutor hurried in,
her face blending into her white-blonde hair as she tried
to give us a lesson we didn't need.

At home I watched the footage, the terrible
path of the first plane followed by the second, the desperate
jumpers like broken seagulls.

I felt a sickening inside, my hand on my mouth
at the senselessness horror,
the ruin of it all – the now, the never, the why.

In bed I revisited my hands, no paler than before.

# 7 July 2005 & after

*Heard what's happened in London?* our boss said
and we thought she meant in our office down there.
I resisted the panic to call my new partner
emailed instead.
*Just heard the news – trust you're okay…?*
and within seconds he replied
in work having missed it by minutes.

The next day was my weekend to visit
but the girl at the counter wouldn't sell me a ticket.
*No one's allowed in* she said with a shrug
so he came up to me instead.

A month later we caught up with a friend
who said she'd been there on business.
She'd failed to board the packed train
felt the blast from the platform.

Two years after
I decided to move in.
I was saying goodbye to a neighbour
when her daughter
big-eyed and listening asked
*Why do you want to move there?*
*That's where they bomb people.*

# The Terracotta Army

I

In the silent room
they all face the same way
each expression different
all with stone hearts.

II

*Where are we going?*
*You'll see. Keep moving.*
*What'll we do when we get there?*
*Fight. For your country. For your King.*
*How'll we know when we've won?*
*There'll be no breath left to take.*

III

One day we will be famous
thousands will flock to see our thousands
watchful and waiting
caught on the threshold of freedom
the door within touching distance.

# The Suicide Net

Fremantle Prison, 1850–1991

It was just getting ridiculous
all the bodies on the floor
(Yorkshire flagstone no less).

Lifers wanting none of it.
Innocents wanting out of it.
The insane wanting it all.

So up it went.

And being taut leftover fence wire
to keep 'out' rather than 'down'
it stopped the mess
stuff only surgeons should see
but not the deaths.

It also stopped the buckets
surprising guards with oblivion
though the contents still made it.

# Shop no. 4

I am what you'll never have.

You want my colour.
I prefer yours.

You say my figure is like a cola bottle
can't believe my age.

I look in your rheumy eyes
find the stretch of your life
the years of here
an exhaustion I'll never know.

And I do as expected –
leave you calling my name.

# City to Seaford

She cries silently, all puff and no sound, just
a steady streaming everybody ignores like
the rush-hour passengers on this train. Except me.

I think back to when I was told my dad had
cancer, in the liver of all places, by my stepsister
who was in pieces on the phone miles away.

Despite the 'C' word and choked sobs, not one
soul on the bus, as it crossed London Bridge, asked
if I was okay. They were all eyes and no mouth.

She swipes at her tears as the landscape flits
by, a reminder time moves quickly and stops
for no one, like the fat pocket watches of crickets.

I hand her a tissue and see her eyes are brushed
silver. I picture our fridge in its frozen song, which
always ends with a shudder, as if it remembers the cold.

# Pay back

They gather in groups
watching you.
You wonder what they're thinking
pray they don't move
don't reach out.

They look lost in their fashion
out of sorts
their faces loom large
like dreams with muddy feet.

You can't stare too much
or you'll have to give them things.
Not just your purse
but all you are
so they can take over your life
and be.

## Reef fishing

They hunt at sunset
when the waters are heavy with the heat of the day
the waves a whisper of their former fury.

They move with purpose
a scatter of colour on sea-spangled outcrops
buckets brimming with what they never take home.

They work until dark
and even then a few continue by torchlight
their arcs and pinpoints like some fallen constellation.

# Balinese pool

I find peace in a Balinese pool
        swathes of water lilies
hide the flash of fish below.

A stone girl reclines in its centre
        frangipani flowers scattered
like worn lovers around her.

A dragonfly zips through
        trailblazing its colour
between a blur of crisp wings.

I crouch to look closer.

What I thought were brown spots
        are fingernail-sized frogs
squatting on lily pads like tiny worries.

I watch a few flick into fathomless depths.

# Run with the colours of home

## Interislander

Listing on blue
we coast from North Island to South.

The Marlborough Sounds
reminds our window where it is
with a fat slap of its hand.

The rusted frame relents
leaks fingers of saltwater
after every reproach.

I finish my sauv blanc
position my glass
to catch each imprint.

# City of cones

New Zealand roads        take extra        time.

They're cracked,
        ripped up or closed.

Christchurch,
the garden city,
        struggles
between ocean and alps.

Lying faultless
on a fault line,
        it's a leftover quake
steeped in the remains
of lost things.

Its heart is dying
from arterial roads no longer feeding.

There's a cultural forgetting
in perpetual recovery,
a sadness heavier
        than a displaced building.

And yet,
pop-up shops and food stalls
are fronted with welcome,

a resilience        forming foundations.

# Bordertown

We agree to freshen up
before eating
dinner being bikie bar burgers.

For us
a quick shake down of dust.

For you
a divine intervention.

You billow in beaming
festooned in white
complete with J sandals tied.

And as Him from Nazareth
command red wine
oblivious to open-mouthed faces.

You set up a game of pool.
We locate our nearest exit.

# Jaipur

was a contradiction.
With the poor in its pockets
it dressed in fine wares,
splashing colour wherever it went.

We checked into a suite in Shapura House
with dark wood and patterned velvet,
and a four-poster bed
I hit my head against one afternoon we had sex.

We bought puppets from a market,
named them Zig and Zag,
practiced the art of giving life.

Part of your tooth fell out over dinner
and when I asked for tea,
they brought me English Breakfast with a smile.

## Fox Glacier

Come, lie down between the Alps with me
rest your feet on the carpeted hills

See the rabbits panting in the shade
the horny stags in the one field
the pretty does in the next
the roses bookending wild vines
the blue bottomless lakes

Come, melt my glacial heart
watch the forest steam as the sun rises

## Adelaide vs Brisbane

*I'll give you the balmy evenings*
*and tropical landscape*
*I'll give you those,*
*oh, and the wonderful lack of mozzies.*
*But we have some of the finest wine regions*
*and of course, Festival time!*

> *Yes, but we're hip ALL of the time,*
> *have more life,*
> *most of which is outdoors,*
> *whereas you'll be shivering come July.*

*Maybe, but at least we have seasons*
*and didn't need to trash our winter wardrobe.*
*Plus, our hills will give your hinterland*
*a run for its money.*
*And, and, we have longer days,*
*no getting dark at six.*

> *Yes, but our days start sooner,*
> *it's light at five-thirty,*
> *enough time for a swim before work.*

*Hmm, okay, but ours is a dry heat,*
*none of this sweating and dripping,*
*you may as well live in your river.*

> *Yes, there is that.*
> *And your airport's easier to get to,*
> *which is handy seeing as you're*
> *pretty much in the middle of nowhere…*

*Talking of nowhere,*
*how close is your nearest beach?*
*Sorry, about an hour you say?*
*Ours is a twenty-minute walk*
*and one of the best around!*

*Aarh, but we have the river.*

*Right back at ya!*

# Jantar Mantar

A sociologist and a poet
visit an astronomical site.

Both are in heaven.
One sees calculation instruments
the other celestial bodies.

They look at each other and smile.

Both find and climb themselves.
One examines two faces
while the other admires neat horns.

Both note the bull in between.

And then to Samrat Yantra
to watch it inch its shadow
the width of a hand every minute.

They reach for each other's
stand in communicable silence.

Samrat Yantra – the world's largest sundial, which measures time in intervals of two seconds using sunlight.

## Snowdonia

In a restaurant in Picton
overlooking the hills
I share a sudden memory with you.

On a school trip to Snowdonia
as I'm gazing at the evening horizon
my English teacher offers me a penny for my thoughts.
I tell him I see a huge hand appear
a giant's hand
gripping the mountains as if to pull himself over.
There's silence as he doesn't answer
simply smiles at the vision I've given.

I leave out the part
how later that weekend
there was an excursion to Barry Island's fair
where I threw up my imagination on the waltzers.

# Bondi to Bronte

I idle through natural beauty
on a clifftop walk
as the ocean slams its power below.
Each turn reveals something delicious
a burst of hibiscus, a velvet cove.
I feel I'm being rinsed of all I don't need,
the inevitable leaving,
knowing you're elsewhere.

She approaches with rhythm,
her silicone tits barely contained,
her long-chiselled legs taper to Nike,
both so unlike my own.
I try to guess her age.
A man keeps pace, brilliantly bronzed.
She pouts her bee-stung lips
as a seagull screams overhead.

Mid-twenties I decide,
he looks a little older.
I step aside, let them pass,
admire cerulean and smile.

# The Oodnadatta Track

## I Woomera first

The road ahead is flooded with heat
a silver that shimmers like thirst on the tongue.
There are warnings of life running wild.
An emu appears – a shock of feathers on legs.
The sun blazes like a mother scolding
as our windscreen weathers small deaths.

## II Moving onto Marla

Our windscreen weathers small deaths
as our air-conditioned eyes sweep fire-red earth.
Scrub gives way to the moonscape of Coober,
craters and mounds for a slipstream of opal.
I balance the sun on my knees as you drive,
look up to catch the blush of galahs.

## III Oodnadatta marks the start

I look up to catch the blush of galahs.
The track reminds us how loose we are
our bodies moving where they gather most.
We stop for tea in a dry creek bed,
your back is alive with flies, my feet swell.
An eagle fans a sky as high as an ocean is wide.

## IV Respite in William Creek

An eagle fans a sky as high as an ocean is wide,
today it is stirred with a dribble of cloud.
A brown snake crosses despite our proximity,
its belly surely singing with warning.
It drapes over a bush like outback tinsel
as we continue in our dance of bones.

## V Maree urges onward

We continue in our dance of bones.
Small birds move like the minutes of an hour.
We reach Lake Eyre through a burnt planet of rock,
its expanse sears the back of our eyes.
You return with salt, snowflake it for me
while dust plumes as if something has ruined.

## VI Home via Leigh Creek

Dust plumes as if something has ruined.
We steal a kiss in shelled rooms of a long-ago town.
Fingers of weather reach for the ranges,
push light to the ground where it will sleep until morning.
Trees stand like leftover witchcraft
as we return to port gleaming like a promise we kept.

# The Taj

Jumping from the rickshaw, we pass
        through ornate outer buildings with purpose.

I'd been dreaming about this since we'd arrived,
        strangely, never before.

As expected it takes my breath away,
        gives it me back in short bursts,

shimmers at the end of a landscaped waterway,
        impossibly bright and singing.

Tagore's description comes to mind –
        *the teardrop on the cheek of time.*

Its moonstone-coloured expanse is dream-like,
        splashed in a rainbow of saris,

with pearl domes and minarets, archways and spires,
        it's art no one photo can frame.

Up close, I trace herringbone inlays, arabesques
        of flowers and vines in jasper and jade, laid bare

for billions of fingers to press heartbeats
        into its marble, hello the dead inside.

Rabindranath Tagore (1861–1941) was a poet and became the voice of India's spiritual heritage.

# Henley Beach

Sky presses Sea
an argument imminent

both vie to look meaner
in gunmetal grey

Air holds its breath
Sun intervenes

is snuffed & shoved aside
Air exhales

tries to keep pace
with the fury building

words are exchanged
lightening quick

& then the first punch
splits space

with a thunderous crack
that leaves ears ringing

# Flight attendant

She collects sunrises
twenty-seven so far
loops them around her wrists
dazzling passengers
when she greets them aboard.

She glides down the aisle
her movements precise
smiles sweetly at the rude man
whips cotton candy from clouds
for the girl who hates flying.

She prepares for landing
puts herself in place after
and as they bank to the right
she plucks another miniature city
for the world behind her eyes.

## Sólfar, Reykjavik

With just five hours of daylight
we leave early for the waterfront.

The sky is still thick with sleep
snug against the sea

the snow-capped mountains silent.
The water is glass

shatters only when it reaches
the shoreline of rock.

We find the sculpture overlooking the bay
pristine on a circle of granite.

A steel boat of sorts
all angles, ice and edges

the stern lifted, as if longing to leave
set sail for someplace else.

It reminds me of a whale
taken, stranded

its soul lamenting the deep.

# Mahjong

He reaches for another tile
his hand steady
looks up at you as you click
to capture their game
wonders what you will do with the image
of the four of them
straight-backed on stone seats
north, south, east and west of a table
under watchful trees
by a listening pool
wondering who you are
why you are here

# Darwinian

She waits at the gate
her skin smooth like the chair she sits on
cross-legged in pink pants
the rest of her lost in an oversized coat.

She looks about ten
in one of the oldest surviving cultures
her left eye patched up
the other long-lashed and defiantly shut.

She counts

       the skin names of her family

             moves in contested middle space

                   footfalls the Dreaming

                         singing through earth

.       forgets how recent events are

   remembers the body

can be read from a distance

       where saltwater meets fresh

             and the self dislocates

   to run with the colours of home

www.ingramcontent.com/pod-product-compliance
Lightning Source LLC
Chambersburg PA
CBHW062148100526
44589CB00014B/1742